EXAMINING POLITICAL SYSTEMS™



# MONARCHY

Xina M. Uhl and Katy Schiel

rosen publishing's
rosen central®
New York

Published in 2020 by The Rosen Publishing Group, Inc.
29 East 21st Street, New York, NY 10010



First Edition



**Library of Congress Cataloging-in-Publication Data**

Names: Uhl, Xina M., author. | Schiel, Katy, author.
Title: Monarchy / Xina M. Uhl and Katy Schiel.
Description: First edition. | New York : Rosen Central, 2020. | Series: Examining political systems | Includes bibliographical references and index. | Audience: Grades 5–8.
Identifiers: LCCN 2018018879| ISBN 9781508185239 (library bound) | ISBN 9781508185222 (pbk.)
Subjects: LCSH: Monarchy—History—Juvenile literature.
Classification: LCC JC375 .U45 2019 | DDC 321/.6—dc23
LC record available at https://lccn.loc.gov/2018018879

*Manufactured in the United States of America*

**On the cover:** Australian newspaper articles celebrate the marriage of Prince William and Kate Middleton in April 2011 (*upper left*); the coronation of Queen Victoria *(lower left)*; and Queen Elizabeth II waves from Buckingham Palace in 2012 (*right*).

# CONTENTS

# INTRODUCTION

Even in modern times, the concept of royalty holds a certain charm. Kings, queens, princesses, and princes bring to mind jewels, crowns, thrones, and the public kneeling before them as if they possessed sacred powers. Many societies throughout history believed that monarchs did possess such powers. The practice of monarchy in diverse forms is the most ancient political system on earth, and has been tried by almost every nation. In its earliest days, even America was ruled by a king. Monarchs have been referred to by different titles over the centuries, including pharaoh, emperor, caesar, czar, and kaiser. Each of these titles means supreme ruler.

Monarchies come in three kinds: absolute, limited, and constitutional. The absolute monarch who holds complete power is the oldest and most common form of monarchy.

Constitutional monarchy involves reducing a monarch's power by a legislative body. England popularized this form of power in the eighteenth century. It survives in a limited, mostly ceremonial fashion, with Queen Elizabeth II. She serves as the United Kingdom's head of state and head of the commonwealth. Though she carries out limited constitutional duties, she is an important symbol of the UK. Most of her functions are ceremonial since Britain's political parties hold the vast majority of the nation's governmental powers. Those monarchies that remain in present times are almost all constitutional in nature.

Queen Elizabeth II rides in a carriage beside her husband, Prince Philip, on May 27, 2015. Queen Elizabeth is the world's longest-reigning monarch, having come to the throne in 1952 after the death of her father, King George VI.

Limited monarchy refers to ruling figureheads who do not hold any power in government. Modern examples include the Danish queen and the Swedish king. They are usually expressions of their countries' traditions instead of strong rulers as in former times.

In the early days of human history, people banded together in small groups to roam the land looking for food and game. Those who were skilled in hunting—and warfare—became the leaders of their people, the earliest monarchs. Over time, humans learned to cultivate grains and settled down to become farmers. A steady food supply allowed for the growth of population and for the building of cities—some of them great and powerful. An excess of food meant that not everyone had to involve themselves in food production as with hunters and gatherers. New occupations developed, such as artisans, priests, and at the top of the social hierarchy, rulers. These early monarchies wielded absolute power. The rule was usually kept within the family whenever possible, passing from father to the eldest son, or occasionally, daughter.

In much of history, a strong, just monarchy was considered the ideal political system. Society functioned best when the monarch provided justice and encouraged a thriving economy. But all too often weak and corrupt monarchs gained power, and the people suffered from their rule.

From the days of ancient Egypt to the dawn of the twenty-first century, the monarchy has thrived. The pages that come tell the stories of these rulers and the people who lived under them.

CHAPTER 1

# THE EARLIEST MONARCHIES (3500–30 BCE)

Ancient Egypt was home to the world's oldest civilizations, which lasted more than three thousand years. Modern historians invented the idea of naming periods to describe particular stretches of time. For example, the period of the Old Kingdom in Egypt ran from about 2700 to 2184 BCE. The fifth dynasty began in 2465 BCE and ended in 2325 BCE. Lasting approximately 140 years, the fifth dynasty was part of the Old Kingdom.

## ANCIENT EGYPTIAN ROYALTY

The kings and queens of ancient Egypt were part of the longest ruling monarchy in history. From about 3500 BCE, when the first of the kings ruled over a united Egypt, to 30 BCE, to when Cleopatra killed herself rather than submit to Roman rule, Egyptian civilization flourished under the leadership of the divine pharaohs.

This ancient Egyptian painting shows the pharaoh between the gods Harseisis (*left*) and Anubis (*right*). Pharaohs were considered gods themselves.

## THE PHARAOHS

The ancient Egyptians believed that they were ruled for many thousands of years by the gods before the first pharaoh, Narmer, came to the throne. Every pharaoh was considered divine, because he was believed to be descended directly from the gods. Since the pharaoh was considered divine, he or she (the pharaohs were most often men, although there were a few very notable queens) possessed absolute power.

As the representative of the gods on earth, the pharaoh was a visible symbol of divine authority. He spoke directly to the people in their temples, dedicated building projects, decided government policy, supervised officials, and led armies into war.

But the Egyptian monarchy was not always strong. Like every administration, it had its good and bad times. Until the fourth dynasty (2550 BCE), pharaonic power enjoyed its golden age. The throne began to lose its power very slowly until it was overtaken by the Romans in 30 BCE.

## KINGS OF MESOPOTAMIA

In 3500 BCE, the two kingdoms of Egypt were united by the legendary first pharaoh, Menes, also known as Narmer. Around the same time in Mesopotamia (present-day Iraq), the Assyrians, Sumerians, and Babylonians rose under a series of powerful monarchs. One of the first and most famous of the Mesopotamian kings, the legendary Gilgamesh, ruled much later in 2700 BCE. During Egypt's long golden age, many other monarchies grew and flourished as other civilizations developed near Egypt. Greece, Rome, Syria, Persia, and Phoenicia all became powerful and established monarchies while Egypt's pharaohs reigned.

Shown here, the Palette of Narmer illustrates events from Narmer's reign. The front of the palette (*left*) depicts men taming wild animals while the back of the palette (*right*) shows Narmer inspecting corpses, most likely enemies slain in battle.

## PALETTES, PAPYRI, AND MORE

The artifacts described in this chapter are a small sampling of the countless discoveries from Ancient Egypt. However, these in particular highlight the importance of the monarch in ancient Egyptian civilization.

# THE PALETTE OF NARMER

The Palette of Narmer was discovered in 1898 by British archaeologist J. E. Quibell in the ancient predynastic capital Hierakonpolis. Unfortunately, the exact circumstances of the find were not recorded, which adds to its mystery. What archaeologists do know is that this flat slab of slate, measuring 25 inches (64 centimeters) high, is carved on both sides with depictions of events and symbols from the reign of King Narmer, or Menes, a very early Egyptian pharaoh. Most historians believe that it dates from about 3000 to 3050 BCE.

Like many artifacts from ancient Egypt, there is much about the Palette of Narmer that is shrouded in mystery. It might only be a slate palette meant for preparing cosmetics, decorated with symbols representing the legendary first king of Egypt, Narmer, and the unification of Upper and Lower Egypt.

However, the substantial weight and decoration of the Palette of Narmer suggests it had more important uses. On it, Narmer wears the crown of Upper Egypt on one side of the palette and the crown of Lower Egypt on the other. This may indicate that he was the king responsible for the merging of Upper and Lower Egypt into a single kingdom.

As we learned from the Palermo Stone, the ancient Egyptians believed that the gods ruled Egypt for many thousands of years before the god Horus is said to have given the throne to the first human king, Menes. Egyptian tradition credits Menes as the king who united the two Egypts. Historians had always considered King Menses a myth, or not a real person (much like the god kings of early Egyptian history). Because of the information on the Narmer Palette, many now believe that perhaps Menes really did exist. Regardless of what its actual meaning is, the Palette of Narmer is one of the most important artifacts relating to Egypt's first dynasty.

## THE PALERMO STONE

One important source of our knowledge about ancient Egypt is the Palermo Stone, a fragment from a large basalt stone tablet inscribed with the names of the early monarchs. Created around 3000 BCE, the Palermo Stone is inscribed on both sides with royal history stretching back to the earliest times.

Found in Egypt in 1866, much of the stone is now housed in the Palermo Archaeological Museum Sicily, Italy. Other pieces of it are in the Cairo Museum in Egypt and the Petrie Museum in London. The original unbroken slab might have been as long as 9 feet (2.7 meters), but we will never know since most of it is missing. In fact, no one knows when and where the stone was found. It was later identified in 1895 by a French scholar who saw it at the Palermo museum and recognized its significance. Until then, many of the references found in ancient Egyptian artifacts were a mystery. The stone's information was the missing piece of the puzzle.

The Palermo Stone recorded the history the of the kings of Lower Egypt, beginning with the thousands of years that Egypt was believed to be ruled by the gods. The history covers the time of the god Horus, who is said to have given the throne to the human king, Menes. Human rulers are listed up to the fifth Dynasty. The history is written in long horizontal rows, divided up into small rectangles, each representing one year. The year boxes, separated by dividing lines, are headed by the name of the king in power at the time. Each year box contains a reference to an event or series of events that took place in that year. The kinds of events recorded on the Palermo Stone are religious ceremonies, taxation information, building records, and wars. The highest level of the Nile is also recorded. The last name preserved on the stone is that of Neferirkare, the third of the nine kings of the fifth dynasty (2465–2325 BCE). The Palermo Stone is a very important document in Egyptian history because it reveals the names of Egypt's early rulers. It has helped historians find their way through the long maze of Egyptian history.

## THE ADMONITIONS OF IPUWER

*The Admonitions of an Egyptian Sage* are the lamentations of an Egyptian sage, Ipuwer, written on papyrus, an early kind of paper. Dating from about 2200 BCE, the narration describes a very bleak time during the first intermediary period of Egypt. Part of the dark ages in Egyptian history, this period began in 2180 BCE and lasted for about a century. The surviving *Admonitions* are a copy of the original, rewritten in Egyptian Demotic (or popular) script on to papyrus that is now tattered with time. It is housed today in the Leiden University in Holland.

Ipuwer, the author of the *Admonitions*, laments an almost complete breakdown of the long-established social order, and calls for the restoration of a powerful monarchy. He paints a horrific scene of mummies speaking from the grave and dead bodies floating down the Nile. There is political unrest across the land, and people no longer feel safe. Ancient documents are being destroyed, and monuments are being smashed. Foreigners have invaded Egypt, and there is no strong leader who can put an end to the suffering and chaos. Ipuwer complains that "hearts are violent, pestilence is throughout the land, blood is everywhere, death is not lacking, and the mummy-cloth speaks even before one comes near it … noblemen are in distress, while the poor man is full of joy." To Ipuwer, the health of the monarchy reflected the health of the society and was the only guarantee of civilization.

Pharaoh Mentuhotep II reunited Egypt after it had been divided by conquest and internal strife for more than a century. Mentuhotep II launched many building projects, the most notable of which is his burial complex, which houses this statue.

## THE MONARCHY ENDS

Around 2055 BCE, the throne of the pharaoh was restored to its glory by Pharaoh Mentuhotep II. This event ushered in the period that came to be known as the Middle Kingdom.

Despite many periods of change, Egyptian monarchs continued to rule and flourish up until the reign of Cleopatra in the first century BCE. Rather than submit to the foreign rule of the Romans, Cleopatra killed herself (according to legend) by allowing a poisonous snake to bite her. The great reign of the pharaohs was now over, but the time of the Roman emperors was just beginning.

CHAPTER 2

# KINGS AND EMPERORS OF ANCIENT ROME (509 BCE–CE 305)

Legend says that a she-wolf suckled the two founders of Rome, Romulus and Remus, when, as babies, their father caused them to be abandoned by a river. Romulus became Rome's earliest king, according to myth. Rome's founding took place in 753 BCE. The reign of the kings came to an end in 509 BCE when Tarquin the Proud, the seventh king of Rome, was deposed for his cruelty. For the next 500 years, the Roman Republic ruled.

## THE ROMAN REPUBLIC

A republic refers to a political structure in which the supreme power is controlled by the body of citizens that is entitled to vote for officers and representatives who are responsible for them. From their early experiences with kings, the Romans had come to despise the monarchy, fearing the effect unlimited power that kings held over human minds.

This first century BCE bust shows Julius Caesar, who reigned as Rome's dictator from 49 BCE until his assassination in 44 BCE by members of the Senate.

As a republic, Rome was governed by two consuls who shared power equally. The consuls, elected every year, were advised by the senate, a group of experienced legislators. The republic was designed to stop a single ruler from ever growing powerful again, but as we shall see, future emperors had other plans.

## THE REPUBLIC FALLS

By 31 BCE, Rome was at the center of an enormously rich empire that stretched across Europe and the Middle East. A republican government had worked well while Rome was a small city, but was not working for an entire empire. Quarrels among rival senators led to a breakdown in the 500-year-old republic. Military leaders such as Julius Caesar (100–44 BCE) began to demand more political power. Caesar was murdered in 44 BCE by a group of republicans led by Cassius and Brutus, who feared that Caesar intended to establish a monarchy, and make himself ruler. Caesar's murder demonstrated the extent of the Romans' hatred for the very idea of monarchy. Although Caesar was murdered by the senators, the political problems in Rome continued.

In 43 BCE Caesar's nephew, Octavian, forced the senate to make him consul. In 31 BCE, he declared himself "first citizen" of Rome. He had become, in effect, a king. In 27 BCE, Octavian became emperor, renaming himself Augustus.

## AGE OF EMPERORS

The age of the Roman emperor had begun. This new breed of emperor who ruled in conjunction with the senate became the model and envy of later European kings.

### TRAJAN AND THE GOLDEN AGE

The Romans eventually accepted the idea of a monarchy. Under Emperor Trajan, who ruled from CE 98 to 117, the Roman Empire expanded to its largest size. From modern Portugal in the west, to modern Kuwait in the east, the British Isles in the north, and modern Sudan in the south, the Roman Empire was the largest in history, and the emperor was placed firmly at the top.

Emperor Trajan was perhaps the most beloved and able of the Roman emperors. He was said to have a majestic and grand appearance. Despite his iron will, he was reported to be extremely kind and chivalrous, famous for his compassionate treatment of the poor. During his reign, the Roman Empire grew to its largest and established many communities. Along with the new Roman communities came order, especially to the "uncivilized" Germanic areas to the north.

Trajan was also a great builder, as evidenced by the many ruins of his public buildings. In addition, he encouraged commerce and industry within the empire. Art and culture flourished during his

This map shows the greatest extent of the Roman Empire in CE 117. Under Emperor Trajan, the empire reached from Britain in the north to Egypt in the south and from Spain in the west to Syria in the east.

rule, and he can be compared to the most enlightened monarchs of the later Italian Renaissance.

Emperor Trajan's rule represents the Golden Age of Rome, a time when there were no military defeats, culture flourished, and the emperor was the supreme leader of 20 million residents throughout the great empire.

## HADRIAN'S WALL

One of the greatest symbols of the power and reach of the Roman emperors still stands in Great Britain. Hadrian's Wall, built in CE 122 runs across 73 miles (117.5 kilometers) of English open countryside, separating the north of Great Britain from the south.

When Trajan died of a stroke in CE 117, Hadrian became emperor. Hadrian, who had his own ideas about the empire, did not want to conquer any new territories. The army, used to being at war, was unhappy with this new policy. In addition, Hadrian, who did not get along with many of the senators, had some of them executed. Hadrian became extremely unpopular.

One of Hadrian's favorite and most often repeated sayings was, "A ruler exists for the State and not the State for the ruler." To this end, Hadrian improved communications within the empire and created an international civil service to administer the community of nations within the Roman Empire. The Roman Empire was at its greatest size and power.

## BUILDING HADRIAN'S WALL

The British Isles had been more or less under Rome's control since 55 BCE, when Julius Caesar invaded the southern coast. After almost 200 years, however, Rome had still failed to conquer the fierce and defiant Celts of the Scottish north.

In CE 122, Hadrian visited Britain and ordered a wall to be built between the Solway Firth in the west and the River Tyne in the east. The wall would "separate Romans from Barbarians."

*(continued on the next page)*

*(continued from the previous page)*

Roman soldiers built the great wall over six years. In addition to being fighting men, these men were often skilled architects, masons, carpenters, and surveyors whose talents are apparent today. The wall is 10 feet (3 m) wide with milecastles, or garrisons, at every mile. Thousands of soldiers were positioned at the wall, keeping watch over windswept and isolated Scotland.

To the "barbarians" of the north, Hadrian's Wall must have seemed an awesome symbol of the strength of the Roman emperor. Even today, the wall remains one of the most spectacular symbols of how far the Roman Empire reached.

This photo shows the remains of Hadrian's Wall in modern times. When intact, the wall stretched for 73 miles (118 km) across the width of northern Britain.

# MARCUS AURELIUS

When he was only a child, Marcus Aurelius attracted the attention of Emperor Hadrian, who appointed the young man to the priesthood. The Emperor Marcus Aelius Aurelius Antoninus (who reigned from CE 161–180) was the only Roman emperor besides Julius Caesar whose writings have become classics of Western literature. He is perhaps the only true "philosopher king" in history.

Although far from a remarkable warrior or administrator, he was well-loved by his people because of his compassion. Marcus Aurelius was a social reformer who worked for the betterment of the poor, slaves, and criminals. He ordered the gladiators to fight with blunted points, so that they would not be seriously injured in a fight.

Anti-Christians in the Western world have often looked to him as a role model since he was a fierce persecutor of Christianity. Marcus Aurelius believed (as most Romans did) that Christianity threatened the values that made Rome great.

Marcus Aurelius was very pious and committed to a system of beliefs known as Stoicism. A

Marcus Aurelius was a pious man committed to the philosophy of Stoicism, which stressed self-discipline and simplicity. His writings, *The Meditations of Marcus Aurelius*, survive and are still widely read.

philosophy that had been popular among the better-educated Romans for hundreds of years, Stoicism stressed self-discipline, simplicity, virtue, and inner tranquility. Stoics did not express emotions or feelings, such as sadness, fear, or happiness. As a teenager, Marcus Aurelius spent a lot of time training himself to be indifferent to hunger, heat, and cold. He slept on bare floors and studied the teachings of the great Stoic thinkers.

*The Meditations of Marcus Aurelius* is a loosely organized collection of his thoughts on stoicism. *Meditations* is a poetic exploration of the mysteries and mysticism of the world. Aurelius worked on them throughout his reign, jotting down a few lines a day, even in the heat of battle.

As emperor, Marcus Aurelius did not impose Stoicism as an imperial religion, as the later Emperor Theodosius imposed Christianity. Had he done so, perhaps today's world would be a very different place.

CHAPTER 3

# MONARCHIES OF THE MIDDLE AGES (CE 500–1300)

The fall of the Roman Empire in around CE 476 brought about the beginning of the European Middle Ages, a period of time that lasted until the fourteenth century. As the ownership of land shifted and consolidated into nation states, monarchs ruled over lands that became rich and powerful.

## EUROPE GROWS

At the beginning of the Middle Ages, Europe as we know it today did not exist. Rather, it was an enormous collection of small areas ruled by lords under the feudal system.

The ideas of the feudal system were based on the shape of a pyramid. A mass of serfs at the base worked to produce wealth for the small number of lords above them.

Serfs were bound to the manor and could not leave it or marry without the manor lord's permission. Serfs, who were uneducated, did all the work on the manor farm. They had small plots of land they could work for themselves. Sometimes a serf could earn enough money to buy his freedom.

A serf offers his master refreshment in this fourteenth-century handbook on health by Tacuinum Sanitatis. Although serfs were not slaves, they were not free and were bound to the land they worked.

A lord or vassal ruled lands granted to them by their king. These lands were called fiefs. Within a fief, a vassal could give portions of his land to vassals of his own. Someone might be the vassal of one person, but the lord of another.

At the top of the pyramid sat the monarch who reaped the wealth created by the serfs below. In return, the monarch provided "protection" from outside invaders. This was a very convenient and lucrative system for the medieval monarchs because it provided them with easy access to wealth and power. Monarchs justified their positions by claiming to possess the divine right to rule bestowed upon them by God. The monarchies of the Middle Ages were the force behind the emergence of the modern nation state, which came into being at the end of the medieval period.

But dynasties came and went quite often, and hereditary power could not be assumed. Establishing legitimacy was a major concern for monarchs. King John of England, for example, failed to establish a strong rule and lost much of his power.

This fifteenth-century painting by Jean Fouquet depicts Charlemagne's coronation on December 25, 800, by Pope Leo III. The pope's act strengthened Charlemagne's rule as Holy Roman Emperor.

## CHARLEMAGNE

Charlemagne, who reigned from CE 768 to 814, was known in his lifetime as the "father of Europe," A Frankish (present-day German) king, Charlemagne was a great patron of artists and scholars. He rescued from oblivion much of the ancient learning of Greece and Rome. He was perhaps the first great monarch of the Middle Ages.

Charlemagne, having converted to Christianity very early in life, had a mission to convert the rest of Europe. It was often a brutal and bloody process. A brilliant and ruthless fighter, he was the first monarch since the fall of the Roman Empire strong enough to unite the lands of Western Europe, which had spent the previous 400 years in chaos. Charlemagne was also able to create the structure for Europe that we know today.

On Christmas Day in 800, as Charlemagne prayed in Saint Peter's Cathedral in Rome, Pope Leo III placed a golden crown on Charlemagne's bowed head, crowning him king of the Holy Roman Empire. This coronation established the legitimacy of Charlemagne's dynasty, which lasted for the next 150 years.

## CHARLEMAGNE'S APPEARANCE

What did Charlemagne look like? The only description we have comes from his friend, the monk Einhard, who wrote:

> *Charles was large and strong and of lofty stature, though not disproportionately tall; the upper part of his head was round, his eyes large and animated, nose a little long, hair fair, and face laughing and merry. He used to wear the national, that is to say the Frank, dress: next to his skin a linen shirt and linen breeches and above these a tunic fringed with silk … he protected his shoulders and chest in the winter by a close fitting coat of otter or marten skins. Overall he flung a blue cloak, and he always had a sword girt about him … the King spent much time and labor … studying rhetoric, dialectics, and especially astronomy … and used to investigate the motions of heavenly bodies most curiously, with an intelligent scrutiny.*

## WILLIAM THE CONQUEROR

After the rule of Charlemagne, it took 200 years for another great monarch to arise in Europe. This was William the Conqueror.

Invading England in 1066, William the Conqueror had himself crowned king on Christmas Day. Although it took until 1072 for him to take over the entire area, he used force and clever planning to establish his legitimacy and strengthen his monarchy.

This section of the Bayeux Tapestry shows William the Conqueror arriving in Bayeux. The tapestry, an embroidery on eight strips of linen, measures 230 feet (70 m) long and 20 inches (51 cm) tall.

William's invasion of England in 1066 is a pivotal moment in history, and the famous Bayeux Tapestry tells its story. A 230-foot (70-meter) long strip of linen embroidered with battle scenes and Latin words, the Bayeux Tapestry describes in pictures William the Conqueror's victory at the Battle of Hastings. In 1066, the Normans (descendants of the Vikings who lived in present-day France) led by Duke William crossed the English Channel and in one vicious battle conquered all of England. William, now "the conqueror," was determined to establish successful control of England. He realized that in order to be accepted as England's legitimate monarch, he would have to respect the laws and

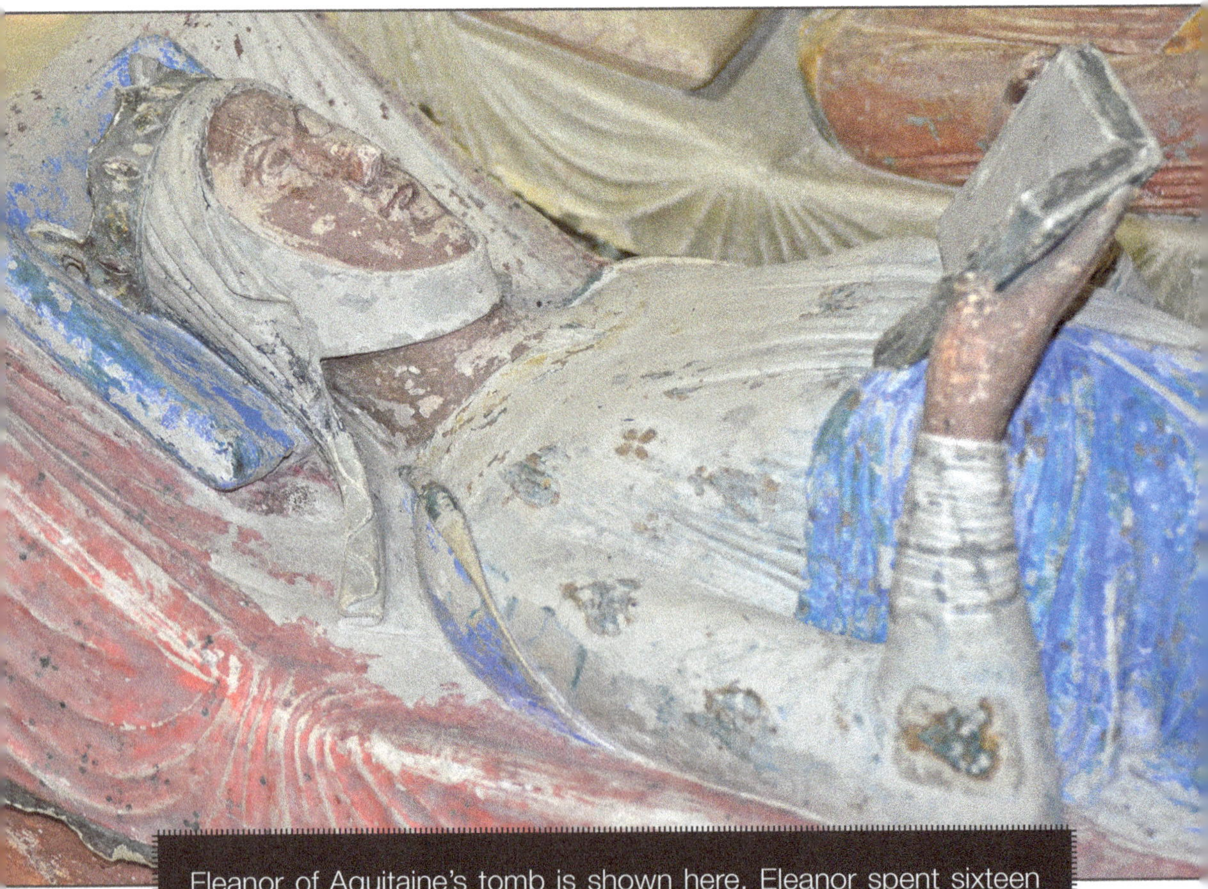

Eleanor of Aquitaine's tomb is shown here. Eleanor spent sixteen years in prison for conspiring with two of her sons to overthrow their father. She ruled England between 1189 and 1199 with the permission of her son King Richard the Lionheart.

traditions of his new people. By preserving the old traditions and skillfully blending new laws with the traditional laws and customs, William was able to convince the conquered Anglo-Saxons to accept him as the legitimate monarch of England. He allowed villages and manors to retain a good deal of autonomy in exchange for military service and monetary payments. This brand of feudalism was seen as an excellent way to strengthen the monarchy. As Britain's first Norman king, William laid the groundwork for Britain's future economic and political success. Always ready for a fight, William was killed in battle in 1087.

## QUEEN ELEANOR

Another strong monarch who ruled both England and France in the Middle Ages was Eleanor of Aquitaine. From 1122 to 1204, Eleanor was one of the most powerful personalities—male or female—of the Middle Ages. She became heir to the vast area of France known as Aquitaine when she was a young girl. At age fifteen, she married the gloomy and severe Louis VII of France, adding large amounts of land to their French holdings. At age nineteen, she offered Bernard of Clairvaux thousands of her vassals to fight in the Second Crusade. Legend states that she appeared at the cathedral of Vézelay on a white horse. Dressed for battle, she urged the crowds to join the crusade. While Bernard was happy for her support, he was less than pleased that she planned to come with 300 of her ladies in waiting. Although Eleanor made it to Jerusalem and back, the pope forbade women from ever participating in the Crusades again.

Eleanor and Louis VII's time together during the Second Crusade proved that they were not well matched, and the marriage was annulled on a technicality. Eleanor's land reverted to her control.

In 1154, Eleanor married Henry, Duke of Normandy (later Henry II, King of England). She bore Henry eight children, two of whom later became kings. Together Eleanor and Henry built an impressive empire through well-crafted alliances, tough fighting, and family connections.

Eleanor was a great patron of the arts, especially music, and she helped to popularize the medieval concept of courtly love. Her grandfather was William IX of Aquitaine, one of the first known troubadours in history. Her support of the medieval troubadour tradition helped place it firmly in the aristocratic courts of France. Eleanor of Aquitaine is an excellent example of the enlightened monarch who used her power to influence the advance of beauty and culture during the Middle Ages.

Even in her old age, Eleanor always traveled. Moving through the kingdoms of Europe, she often risked her life to maintain the loyalty of her subjects, to form marriage alliances, and to manage her army and estates. In her later years Eleanor became known as the "grandmother of Europe."

## KING JOHN

While monarchs were the absolute and unquestioned rulers of their kingdoms, there were times when their subjects rose up against them to question their claim of divine rule. King John of England, grandson of Eleanor of Aquitaine, was considered an unjust and greedy ruler, mostly because of his excessive use of taxes to fund his Third Crusade. In addition, his barons saw him as weak and sneaky, and he fought continuously with his family.

In 1215, a rebellious group of barons took up arms against King John and presented a list of demands that would limit his authority. King John reluctantly signed this list to make peace, but he did not keep his word. The result was civil war in England, during which he was killed. The document, however, which

Drafted and signed nearly eight hundred years ago, the Magna Carta is still considered one of history's most influential documents. See pages 50–51 for a partial transcription.

became known as the Magna Carta, or the "Great Charter," is considered one of the cornerstones of liberty.

The Magna Carta contained several important elements. It gave the Church of England the final word on the selection of people for powerful positions. It prevented a king from demanding more than a reasonable amount of money to run the government without the consent of feudal tenants. Most important, the Magna Carta gave to the nobility the power to limit the king's actions through the use of a written grant. And it gave people the right to a fair trial.

Four copies of the Magna Carta survive. Two are stored at the British Library while the others are preserved in the cathedral archives at Lincoln and Salisbury in the United Kingdom.

CHAPTER 4

# MONARCHS IN THE RENAISSANCE AND EARLY MODERN EUROPE (1400–1750)

From the dawn of the fifteenth century to the middle of the eighteenth century, monarchies in Europe underwent a golden age. The Renaissance, which started in Italy, produced an unparalleled explosion of art, music, architecture, and philosophy. This age also saw European monarchs establishing colonies and seeking to increase their trade wealth.

## ITALIAN MONARCHS

At the end of the Middle Ages, Italy was enjoying a rebirth of art and culture known as the Renaissance. Artists and thinkers such as Leonardo da Vinci and Michelangelo produced history-changing works under the patronage of the Italian monarchs.

The Medicis were a family of Italian bankers who came to the Italian monarchy around 1434. Although they were powerful monarchs, they also had a strong family tradition of artistic patronage and talent.

## LORENZO THE MAGNIFICENT

Lorenzo de Medici (1449–1492), or "Lorenzo the Magnificent," was a statesman, ruler, and patron of the arts. Among his many contributions to Florentine culture was the generous support he gave to such Renaissance geniuses as Leonardo da Vinci and Michelangelo. The Italian writer Niccolò Machiavelli called Lorenzo Medici "the greatest patron of literature and art that any prince has ever been." In his highly influential treatise *The Prince*, Machiavelli used Lorenzo as the perfect example of a strong leader. Lorenzo was an aspiring artist in his own right. He was said to be a decent poet and his works, along with those of the philosopher king Marcus Aurelius, serve as an example of the artistic contributions that monarchs can leave to humanity.

This bronze medal from 1490 shows a side view of Lorenzo de Medici. Lorenzo is considered the most brilliant member of the Medici family; he is remembered as a generous patron of the arts.

## A CLASSIC FOR THE AGES

More than five hundred years ago, Niccolò Machiavelli penned a book that continues to be relevant in the modern world. In *The Prince* (1513), Machiavelli provides a short, readable manual for those seeking power. It advises the "prince," or powerseeker, about how to treat enemies and how to suppress local unrest and partisan squabbling. Machiavelli urges the ruler on how to use force, fraud, and one's friends ruthlessly to attain his desires. Machiavelli counseled the prince to keep power as opposed to fulfilling ideals. He discusses how the use of fear—among both friends and enemies—can provide many benefits. He also originated the concept that the ends should justify the means. In other words, do what you have to do to accomplish something, no matter how distasteful or immoral, because your goal will ultimately be good for the people. Ideas such as this have caused many critics to accuse Machiavelli of being evil.

In an interview with *The New York Times*, Pulitzer-prize winning author Jared Diamond comments about *The Prince*: "[It says that] when you injure someone, do it in a way so that he cannot take revenge. Cultivate an enemy so you can intimidate others by crushing them publicly. It is natural and normal to take territories that do not belong to you." While some object to the ruthlessness of this approach, Diamond argues instead that Machiavelli is a "a crystal-clear realist who understands the limits and uses of power."

## LOUIS XIV

In France, Louis XIV, who ruled from 1643 to 1715, became the model and envy of other European monarchs. During his

Elizabeth I is widely regarded as one of England's most powerful and successful monarchs. During her reign, England increased its colonial holdings and its stature as a world power.

long reign, Louis XIV established nearly absolute control of the government and church. Kings and queens in Spain, Austria, Russia, and Prussia, from around 1650 to the early nineteenth century, all tried to follow his lead. Frederick the Great of Prussia (ruled 1740–1786) and Catherine the Great of Russia (ruled 1762–1796) were strong rulers. But they failed to equal Louis XIV in power.

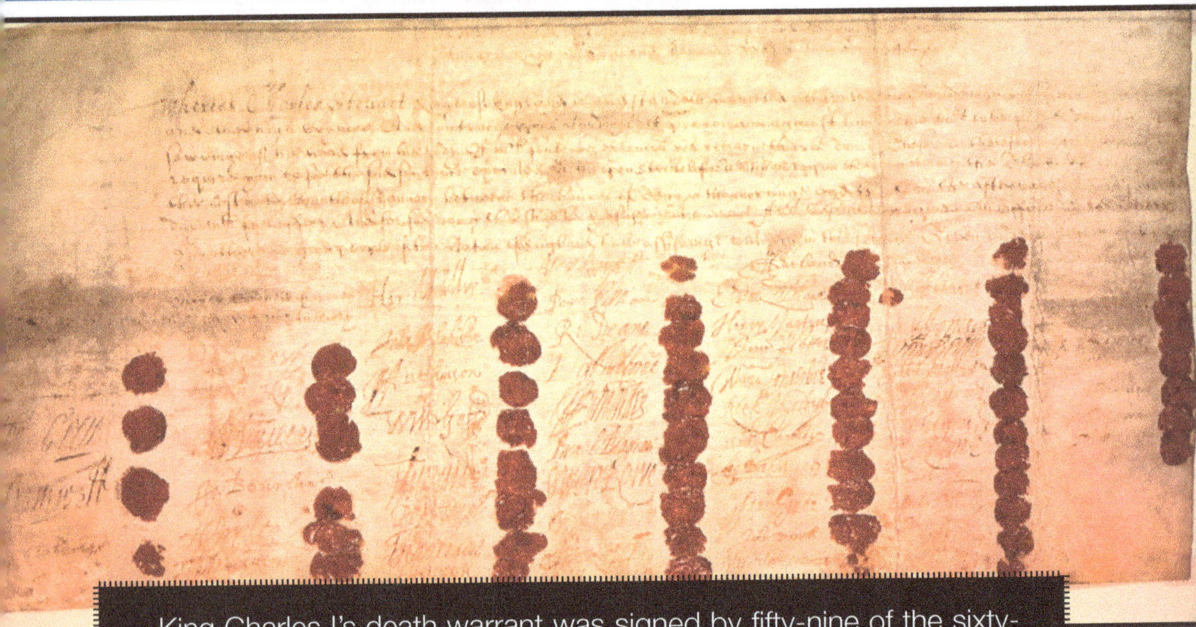

King Charles I's death warrant was signed by fifty-nine of the sixty-seven judges of the High Court of Justice. He was charged with treason. A partial transcription of the January 29, 1649, document appears on pages 51–52.

# ENGLISH ROYALTY

During this period, the English monarchy saw both the expansion of its power with the long and prosperous reign of Queen Elizabeth I (1558–1603) and the contraction of its power with the beheading of Charles I for treason in 1649. Constitutional monarchy was finally established in England with the Glorious Revolution of 1688.

## CHARLES I OF ENGLAND

Unlucky Charles I of England, who reigned from 1625 to 1649, was a strong believer in absolute monarchy and in his own divine right to rule. These beliefs had been passed down to him through his family and from history. But unlike his predecessors, Charles was not allowed to get away with his very undemocratic actions.

After the English Civil War (1630–1660), which had torn apart England and killed countless people, Charles defied the wishes of his people and of Parliament by resuming hostilities with Scotland. Accused of being a traitor and a tyrant, he was put on trial in January 1649. Even during the trial, Charles refused to take his hat off before the judges, reinforcing their perception of him as an arrogant tyrant. He was found guilty.

Before his execution in 1649, Charles addressed the crowd, saying "I have delivered to my conscience; I pray God you do take those courses that are best for the good of the kingdom and your own salvation." With those words, he became the first and only English monarch to be beheaded for treason.

Witnesses claimed that as his head rolled, a huge groan was heard from the crowd. Afterward, people were allowed to approach the body. Many dipped their handkerchiefs in his blood, for the blood of a king, even an unpopular one, was supposed to contain a piece of the divine.

## ABOLISHED AND RESTORED

Only seven days after the execution of Charles I, the institution of monarchy was abolished in England. Parliament determined that "the office of the king in this nation is unnecessary, burdensome, and dangerous to the liberty, society, and public interest of the people." The Council of State was set up, with Oliver Cromwell as the leader.

But the monarchy could not be destroyed so easily. When Charles II returned to become king of England in 1660, during what is now known as the Restoration, the judges who had signed his father's death warrant were tried as regicides (the murderers of a king) and executed. The monarchy was now safely back in control, although its powers were to be permanently lessened in 1689 when the Glorious Revolution established a constitutional monarchy.

# THE REIGN OF LOUIS XIV

If one building symbolizes the grandeur and decadence of absolute monarchy and the "ancient regime" (the old order), it is the Palace of Versailles in France. It was built by the "Sun King," Louis XIV of France, who reigned from 1643 to 1715.

Louis, who had inherited an extremely prosperous country, was able to grasp minute details of the nature of kingship. No other monarch in history has understood as well as Louis XIV the symbolic functions of being a king. The foundation of his

The Hall of Mirrors from the Royal Palace of Versailles is shown here. In this room, the most famous in the palace, the Treaty of Versailles was signed on June 28, 1919, to end World War I.

system was to make a distinction between real power and ceremonial grandeur.

Instead of giving his ministers real power, he granted them symbolic power that depended on his final word. Denying the nobles of actual power, instead he accorded them endless decorative honors to give the illusion of worth and significance. This kept the nobility busy while the king held all of the true power. Louis XIV is famous for saying "L'etat c'est moi," or "I am the state," which sums up how he felt about his position. When he assumed power at age twenty-three, he shocked the world by declaring that he would rule France alone.

Louis hated Paris, preferring to live at the Palace of Versailles, an opulent palace that housed his entire court. At Versailles, etiquette and the pleasure of the king ruled above all else. French nobles and courtiers were expected to come to Versailles to await passing glances from the king. Louis, who had a phenomenal memory, complained if he did not see someone in attendance. Versailles had countless galleries, but nobles were forbidden from discussing politics since informers haunted the halls.

Lavish and time-consuming formalities—hunting, masked balls, and billiards—filled the days and nights of the court of Versailles. In this way, Louis was able to keep the well-educated but powerless elites at his mercy during his fifty-five-year reign.

His descendants, however, were not so lucky. Louis XVI and his wife, Marie Antoinette, reigned over a much more dangerous time for the monarchy.

CHAPTER 5

# MONARCHIES DWINDLE (1789–PRESENT)

Most monarchies cultivated the idea that ordinary people should not question the divine institution of their rule. Yet that idea was turned around in the eighteenth century. English citizens of the American colonies like Thomas Paine challenged the actions of their monarch, King George III in England. The American Revolution, when it came, inspired similar revolutions in other countries such as France.

## REVOLUTION IN FRANCE

Eventually the French monarchy ran out of money. Louis XIV had spent a fortune building the palace at Versailles, Louis XV had wasted millions on his own pleasures, and Louis XVI had given tremendous amounts to help American colonies fight off the British in the American Revolution.

In 1789 Louis XVI called together the Estates-General for the first time since 1614. He was hoping to raise money. The Estates-General was a ruling body created to represent all the people

On July 14, 1789, an angry mob of French peasants forced its way into the Bastille, a prison where the king held political dissidents. The mob released the prisoners and destroyed the building.

of France, even the poorest. Members of the First Estate were the clergy. Second Estate members were the nobles. The Third Estate, which made up more than 95 percent of the population, comprised the workers, poor, and oppressed people of France.

When the Estates-General came together, several things happened. Members of the first two estates, who were expecting the king to give them new political power, were furious when Louis XVI announced he was now expecting them to pay taxes.

Until that time, only people of the Third Estate, the poorest, had paid taxes to the king. In addition, the nobles and clergy refused to admit the representatives of the Third Estate into the meeting. Outraged, members of the Third Estate declared themselves the National Assembly. They met on June 20, 1789 on the tennis court at Versailles, took the "Tennis Court Oath," and drew up plans to run a constitutional government.

## THE RIGHTS OF MAN

The seven articles of the Declaration of the Rights of Man and of the Citizen were adopted by the National Assembly in 1789. See pages 52–54 for a transcription.

*The Declaration of the Rights of Man and of the Citizen* was a revolutionary manifesto drafted by Abbé Emmanuel Sieyès in 1789 and adopted on August 26, 1789, by France's National Assembly. Two years later, in 1791, the declaration was attached as the preamble to France's new constitution. It defined a number of inalienable rights to be enjoyed by all men. This revolutionary pronouncement cancelled the divine right of kings to rule, which had been the basis for French government and social structure since the Middle Ages.

Several articles dealt with abolition of the monarchy while others addressed the rights of the common man to enjoy liberty and security, to own property, and to be free from oppression.

Confusion and hysteria grew intense. It became clear that the three Estates, which had very different ideas and needs, would be unable to agree on guidelines that would benefit everyone. The king was unable or uninterested in helping the groups find a common ground. In the end, his disregard for his people set in motion the French Revolution.

## EXECUTION OF KING LOUIS XVI

In 1793, four years after the declaration was written and the revolution began, Louis XVI and Queen Marie Antoinette were beheaded on the guillotine. It was a huge turning point in European history. Although this was the end of the old French monarchy, a new monarchy, modeled after the ancient Roman emperors, was briefly established by Napoléon in 1799.

## NAPOLÉON BONAPARTE THE DESPOT

"Bonapartism" is a word used to describe despotism, a government or political system in which a ruler with popular consent exercises absolute power. After the French Revolution, France disintegrated into anarchy. The people once again looked for a leader who could bring order and stability. They found it in Napoléon Bonaparte (1769–1821) who rose from obscurity to military greatness, winning the love of the French people. In 1804, Napoléon crowned himself emperor, overriding the ideals of the *Declaration of the Rights of Man and the Citizen.* But he was tyrannical, cruel, and overly ambitious. After a series of disastrous defeats trying to conquer Europe, he was defeated for the last time in 1815 at Waterloo. Napoléon was exiled to a small island where he died.

# THE FADING MONARCHIES

With the nineteenth century came the industrial revolution. Huge numbers of people moved from the countryside to the cities to work in factories. Contact with new people, places, and ideas, caused many Europeans to question the divine right of the monarchs. This led to many upheavals in government structures.

But while movements toward constitutional rule were on the rise from 1789 to 1917, European colonialism was running rampant around the world, with monarchs squarely at the helm. By 1914, Spain, Germany, England, Holland, France, and Portugal controlled almost half of the world.

Although there were still some popular and effective kings and queens, hereditary monarchy as an institution was beginning to die out. The authority of kings and queens was increasingly replaced by parliaments and elected prime ministers.

By the end of World War I, monarchy as it had been known for much of history had nearly disappeared. The Russian Revolution in 1917 brought a violent and bloody end to the reign of the czars. Elsewhere in Europe, monarchs' powers had dwindled to become only a symbol.

## KAISER WILHELM II

Kaiser Wilhelm II (reigned 1888–1918) was the last German monarch and a symbol of European imperialist power. Unlike his relatives on the English throne (Queen Victoria was his grandmother), Wilhelm was no mere figurehead. As the most powerful leader in Europe at the turn of the twentieth century, Wilhelm was in an enviable, but dangerous position.

A brash leader, one of his first actions in 1890 was to dismiss the powerful Chancellor Bismarck—the man responsible for uniting Germany. He then pursued a contradictory and almost suicidal

After his abdication, Kaiser Wilhelm II, in this 1880 photo, went into exile in Holland, where he spent the rest of his life. Holland refused to turn him over to be tried for war crimes at the end of World War I.

foreign policy of aggression toward Russia and France.

What the kaiser wanted more than anything was "a place in the sun" for the German people. This meant he wanted more colonies and more power for Germany. His desire for more *weltpolitik*, or political power in the world, fueled the nationalist sentiments of the German people and ultimately led to World War I.

The war was a disaster for the German people, and for the kaiser as well. By 1918, Germany had gone from being the top power with an enviable standard of living to a chaotic and demoralized state. Kaiser Wilhelm abdicated his throne in November 1918. The German monarchy was finished.

## THE END OF THE CZAR

In 1917, near the end of World War I, another monarchy was coming to an end. But this one ended quite differently. Czar Nicholas II of Russia, who reigned from 1894 to 1917, was a private man who never seemed to hold much interest in being king. Although an absolute monarch, he was weak and ineffective. When there was a popular uprising in 1905, he refused to listen to the people or create reforms that would lessen the burdens of the country's destitute population.

During the war with Kaiser Wilhelm's Germany, however, civil war broke out and the Bolsheviks led by Vladimir Lenin took control of Russia. The Bolsheviks were radicals who thought violent overthrow of the monarchy was better than gradual, democratic change.

Nicholas was forced to abdicate his throne, but it was too late. The Bolsheviks captured the entire royal family and confined them to a house in the city of Ekaterinaburg.

The czar was an important symbol in Russia, and as long as he was alive, the Bolsheviks would be vulnerable to plans to oust their government and restore the monarchy. Since the czar was related to the royal families of Britain, Germany, and Austria, it was likely that they would interfere. There was a possibility that once the war ended, the Western powers would send troops to liberate the imprisoned czar with the

Emperor Hirohito was Japan's monarch during World War II. Japan's defeat in the war marked the decline of the Japanese monarchy. Although Hirohito was allowed to remain on the throne, his role and the monarchy itself became symbolic.

intention of returning him to his throne. But that wasn't to be. With this fear in mind, the Bolshevik leaders made the decision to execute the entire Russian royal family in July 1918. The last Russian czar was dead.

## TODAY'S MONARCHIES

On June 2, 1953, millions of people watched as the teenage Elizabeth II paraded through the streets of London to her coronation. The fate of England did not rest on her shoulders, and she would make no political decisions during her reign. Even so, many people continue to be intensely interested in her

This March 14, 2017, photo shows President Donald Trump and the deputy crown prince of Saudi Arabia, Mohammad bin Salman, during a meeting in the White House's Oval Office.

and her family. Why are we so fascinated with royalty even to modern times?

In Sweden, King Carl Gustaf XVI presently holds reign over a progressive society. Although he holds no political power, he is a powerful and well-loved symbol of the country. Prince Albert II of the tiny European country of Monaco wields power despite the fact that Monaco is a constitutional monarchy. Most of today's approximately thirty surviving monarchies are constitutional monarchies.

The monarchy that rules Saudi Arabia, however, wields more power. Rule is open to members of the Sa'ud family. While the king holds absolute power, it is tempered by the fact that he needs the support of thousands of members of the royal family. Princes occupy the most important government positions. While the kingdom lacks a written constitution, in 1992 the king issued a document of government guidelines known as the Basic Law of Government. Sharia law, or Islamic law, forms the basis of the country's legal and justice systems. Only a small proportion of the population can participate in the political process, no political parties are allowed, and voting does not take place for national bodies. In 2015, King Salman took the throne after the death of his brother Abdullah.

# TIMELINE

**3500 BCE** The two kingdoms of Egypt are united.

**753–509 BCE** The Roman kings rule.

**30 BCE** Cleopatra dies; the age of the pharaohs ends in Egypt.

**27 BCE** The first Roman emperor Octavian Augustus rules.

**CE 122** Hadrian's Wall is constructed.

**161–180** Marcus Aurelius reigns over Rome.

**800** Charlemagne is crowned emperor of the Holy Roman Empire.

**1066** The Battle of Hastings is fought in England.

**1215** The Magna Carta is signed by King John in England.

**1513** Machiavelli's *The Prince* is published in Italy.

**1643** Louis XIV reigns in France.

**1789** The French Revolution breaks out.

**1888** Kaiser Wilhelm II reigns in Germany.

**1918** Nicholas II is executed by the Bolsheviks in Russia.

**1953** Queen Elizabeth II of England is crowned.

**2015** Crown Prince Salman becomes king of Saudi Arabia.

## THE ADMONITIONS OF IPUWER

**Transcription Excerpt**

II

Indeed, poor men have become owners of wealth, and he who could not make sandals for himself is now a possessor of riches. Indeed, men's slaves, their hearts are sad, and magistrates do not fraternize with their people when they shout. Indeed, [hearts] are violent, pestilence is throughout the land, blood is everywhere, death is not lacking, and the mummy-cloth speaks even before one comes near it. Indeed, many dead are buried in the river; the stream is a sepulcher and the place of embalmment has become a stream.

Indeed, noblemen are in distress, while the poor man is full of joy. Every town says: "Let us suppress the powerful among us." Indeed, men are like ibises. Squalor is throughout the land, and there are none indeed whose clothes are white in these times ...

Indeed, the river is blood, yet men drink of it. Men shrink from human beings and thirst after water. Indeed, gates, columns and walls are burnt up, while the hall of the palace stands firm and endures. Indeed, the ship of [the southerners] has broken up; towns are destroyed and Upper Egypt has become an empty waste.

## MAGNA CARTA

**Transcription Excerpt**

(1) FIRST, THAT WE HAVE GRANTED TO GOD, and by this present charter have confirmed for us and our heirs in perpetuity, that the English Church shall be free, and shall have its rights undiminished, and its liberties unimpaired. That we wish this so to be observed, appears from the fact that of our own free will, before the outbreak of the present dispute between us and our barons, we granted and

confirmed by charter the freedom of the Church's elections - a right reckoned to be of the greatest necessity and importance to it - and caused this to be confirmed by Pope Innocent III. This freedom we shall observe ourselves, and desire to be observed in good faith by our heirs in perpetuity.

(9) Neither we nor our officials will seize any land or rent in payment of a debt, so long as the debtor has movable goods sufficient to discharge the debt. A debtor's sureties shall not be distrained upon so long as the debtor himself can discharge his debt. If, for lack of means, the debtor is unable to discharge his debt, his sureties shall be answerable for it. If they so desire, they may have the debtor's lands and rents until they have received satisfaction for the debt that they paid for him, unless the debtor can show that he has settled his obligations to them.

(40) To no one will we sell, to no one deny or delay right or justice.

(63) IT IS ACCORDINGLY OUR WISH AND COMMAND that the English Church shall be free, and that men in our kingdom shall have and keep all these liberties, rights, and concessions, well and peaceably in their fullness and entirety for them and their heirs, of us and our heirs, in all things and all places for ever.

Both we and the barons have sworn that all this shall be observed in good faith and without deceit. Witness the abovementioned people and many others.

Given by our hand in the meadow that is called Runnymede, between Windsor and Staines, on the fifteenth day of June in the seventeenth year of our reign (i.e. 1215: the new regnal year began on 28 May).

## DEATH WARRANT OF KING CHARLES I

**Transcription**

At the high Co[ur]t of Justice for the tryinge and judginge of Charles Steuart Kinge of England January xxixth Anno D[omi]ni 1648.

Whereas Charles Steuart Kinge of England is and standeth convicted attaynted and condemned of High Treason and other high Crymes, And sentence uppon Saturday last was pronounced against him by this Co[ur]t to be putt to death by the severinge of his head from his body Of w[hi]ch sentence execuc[i]on yet remayneth to be done, These are therefore to will and require you to see the said sentence executed In the open Streete before Whitehall uppon the morrowe being the Thirtieth day of this instante moneth of January betweene the houres of Tenn in the morninge and Five in the afternoone of the same day w[i]th full effect And for soe doing this shall be yo[u]r sufficient warrant And these are to require All Officers and Souldiers and other the good people of this Nation of England to be assistinge unto you in this service Given under o[ur] hands and Seales

## DECLARATION OF THE RIGHTS OF MAN AND OF THE CITIZEN

### Transcription

*Approved by the National Assembly of France, August 26, 1789*
The representatives of the French people, organized as a National Assembly, believing that the ignorance, neglect, or contempt of the rights of man are the sole cause of public calamities and of the corruption of governments, have determined to set forth in a solemn declaration the natural, unalienable, and sacred rights of man, in order that this declaration, being constantly before all the members of the Social body, shall remind them continually of their rights and duties; in order that the acts of the legislative power, as well as those of the executive power, may be compared at any moment with the objects and purposes of all political institutions and may thus be more respected, and, lastly, in order that the grievances of the citizens, based hereafter upon simple and incontestable principles, shall tend to the maintenance of the constitution and redound to the happiness of all. Therefore the National Assembly recognizes and proclaims, in the presence and under the auspices of the Supreme Being, the following rights of man and of the citizen:

Articles:

1. Men are born and remain free and equal in rights. Social distinctions may be founded only upon the general good.
2. The aim of all political association is the preservation of the natural and imprescriptible rights of man. These rights are liberty, property, security, and resistance to oppression.
3. The principle of all sovereignty resides essentially in the nation. No body nor individual may exercise any authority which does not proceed directly from the nation.
4. Liberty consists in the freedom to do everything which injures no one else; hence the exercise of the natural rights of each man has no limits except those which assure to the other members of the society the enjoyment of the same rights. These limits can only be determined by law.
5. Law can only prohibit such actions as are hurtful to society. Nothing may be prevented which is not forbidden by law, and no one may be forced to do anything not provided for by law.
6. Law is the expression of the general will. Every citizen has a right to participate personally, or through his representative, in its foundation. It must be the same for all, whether it protects or punishes. All citizens, being equal in the eyes of the law, are equally eligible to all dignities and to all public positions and occupations, according to their abilities, and without distinction except that of their virtues and talents.
7. No person shall be accused, arrested, or imprisoned except in the cases and according to the forms prescribed by law. Any one soliciting, transmitting, executing, or causing to be executed, any arbitrary order, shall be punished. But any citizen summoned or arrested in virtue of the law shall submit without delay, as resistance constitutes an offense.
8. The law shall provide for such punishments only as are strictly and obviously necessary, and no one shall suffer punishment except it be legally inflicted in virtue of a law passed and promulgated before the commission of the offense.
9. As all persons are held innocent until they shall have been declared guilty, if arrest shall be deemed indispensable, all harshness not essential to the securing of the prisoner's person shall be severely repressed by law.

10. No one shall be disquieted on account of his opinions, including his religious views, provided their manifestation does not disturb the public order established by law.
11. The free communication of ideas and opinions is one of the most precious of the rights of man. Every citizen may, accordingly, speak, write, and print with freedom, but shall be responsible for such abuses of this freedom as shall be defined by law.
12. The security of the rights of man and of the citizen requires public military forces. These forces are, therefore, established for the good of all and not for the personal advantage of those to whom they shall be intrusted.
13. A common contribution is essential for the maintenance of the public forces and for the cost of administration. This should be equitably distributed among all the citizens in proportion to their means.
14. All the citizens have a right to decide, either personally or by their representatives, as to the necessity of the public contribution; to grant this freely; to know to what uses it is put; and to fix the proportion, the mode of assessment and of collection and the duration of the taxes.
15. Society has the right to require of every public agent an account of his administration.
16. A society in which the observance of the law is not assured, nor the separation of powers defined, has no constitution at all.
17. Since property is an inviolable and sacred right, no one shall be deprived thereof except where public necessity, legally determined, shall clearly demand it, and then only on condition that the owner shall have been previously and equitably indemnified.

# GLOSSARY

**BASALT** A hard, dense, dark igneous rock that often has a glassy appearance.

**CORONATION** The act of crowning a monarch.

**CRUSADES** A series of military expeditions undertaken by European Christians during the eleventh, twelfth, and thirteenth centuries to recover the Holy Land from the Muslims.

**DYNASTY** A succession of rulers from the same family or line.

**GARRISON** A military post.

**INALIENABLE** Incapable of being removed or transferred to another.

**INDUSTRIAL REVOLUTION** The period between the late eighteenth and early twentieth centuries during which many nations underwent a radical transformation from farm-based to factory-based societies.

**LIBERTY** The right to freedom to engage in certain actions or express certain beliefs without control or interference from the government.

**PAPYRUS** An early paper made from the pith or the stems of an aquatic plant. Used especially by the ancient Egyptians, Greeks, and Romans.

**RENAISSANCE** The period in European history from the fourteenth through the middle of the seventeenth centuries during which there was a revival of classical art, architecture, literature, and learning.

**REPUBLIC** A political system in which the head of state is not a monarch and in which the supreme power lies in a body of citizens who are entitled to elect representatives responsible to them.

**STOICISM** A way of thinking, or a philosophy, that flourished in Ancient Greece in which people felt that, to attain happiness and wisdom, they must restrain their emotions. They refused to show joy or sorrow.

**TROUBADOUR** A twelfth- or thirteenth-century lyric poet in southern France, northern Italy, and northern Spain, who composed and sang songs, often about courtly love.

# FOR MORE INFORMATION

American Independence Museum
One Governors Lane
Exeter, NH 03833
(603) 772-2622
Website: https://www.independencemuseum.org
Facebook: @americanindependencemuseum
The museum educates, studies, and celebrates the people, places, and events that led to the founding of the United States.

Canadian Museum of History
100 Laurier Street
Gatineau, Quebec K1A 0M8
Canada
(800) 555-5621
Website: http://www.historymuseum.ca
Facebook, Twitter, and Instagram: @CanMusHistory
The museum features exhibits on the government and founding of Canada.

Canadian War Museum
1 Vimy Place
Ottawa, Ontario K1A 0M8
Canada
(800) 555-5621
Website: http://www.warmuseum.ca
Facebook: @warmuseum
Twitter: @CanWarMuseum
Instagram: @canwarmuseum
This museum features Canada's involvement in armed conflicts and its interaction with monarchies in Britain.

Colonial Williamsburg
101 Visitor Center Drive
Williamsburg, VA 23185
(888) 965-7254
Website: http://www.history.org/index.cfm
Facebook: @ColonialWilliamsburg
Twitter and Instagram: @colonialwmsburg
A living history museum, this attraction features buildings, artifacts, and guides in period clothing to bring to life Colonial America while the country still lived under a monarchy.

Iolani Palace
364 South King Street
Honolulu, HI 96813
(808) 522-0822
Website: http://www.iolanipalace.org
The only official palace in the United States, this museum features the residence of the Hawaiian monarchs from the late nineteenth century.

Library of Congress
101 Independence Avenue, SE
Washington, DC 20540
(202) 707-5000
Website: http://www.loc.gov
Facebook: @libraryofcongress
Twitter and Instagram: @librarycongress
Multiple collections reveal American history in art, documents, and artifacts from the exploration to the political foundation of the Americas.

# FOR FURTHER READING


Blohm, Craig E. *The Palace of Versailles*. San Diego, CA: ReferencePoint Press, 2015.

Duignan, Brian. *Forms of Government and the Rise of Democracy*. New York, NY: Rosen Publishing, 2013.

Gelletly, LeeAnne. *Monarchy.* Broomall, PA Mason Crest, 2013.

Klar, Jeremy. *The French Revolution, Napoléon, and the Republic: Liberté, Égalité, Fraternité.* New York, NY: Britannica Educational Publishing, 2016.

Levy, Janey. *The Magna Carta.* New York, NY: Gareth Stevens Publishing, 2014.

Lowery, Zoe. *The American Revolution.* New York, NY: Rosen Publishing, 2016.

Nagle, Jeanne. *Feudalism, Monarchies, and Nobility*. New York, NY: Britannica Educational Publishing, 2015.

Perkins, Anne. *Trailblazers in Politics*. New York, NY: Rosen Publishing, 2015.

Santillian, Beatriz. *Leonidas I: Warrior King of Sparta.* New York, NY: Rosen Publishing, 2018.

Witmer, Scott. *Political Systems*. Oxford, UK: Capstone Global Library Ltd., 2013.

# BIBLIOGRAPHY


Ancient Egypt. "The Admonitions of Ipuwer." Retrieved on May 14, 2018. http://www.reshafim.org.il/ad/egypt/texts/ipuwer.htm.

British Library. "The Death Warrant of Charles I." https://www.bl.uk/collection-items/charles-i-death-warrant.

British Library. "English Translation of Magna Carta." July 28, 2014. https://www.bl.uk/magna-carta/articles/magna-carta-english-translation.

Dodson, Aidan. *Monarchs of the Nile*. Cairo, Egypt: The American University in Cairo Press, 2000.

Johnson, Paul. *The Civilization of Ancient Egypt.* New York, NY: HarperCollins, 1999.

Nicolson, Harold. *Kings, Courts, and Monarchy*. New York, NY: Simon & Schuster, 1962.

MacDonald, Fiona. *Timelines: Kings and Queens*. New York, NY: Franklin Watts, 1995.

O'Rourke, John. "Machiavelli's *The Prince*: Still Relevant after All These Years." BU, February 2, 2013. http://www.bu.edu/today/2013/machiavelli-the-prince-still-relevant-after-all-these-years.

Shaw, Ian, ed. *The Oxford History of Ancient Egypt.* New York, NY: Oxford University Press, 2000.

# INDEX

# ABOUT THE AUTHORS

Xina M. Uhl discovered her love of history while still in grade school. She went on to obtain a master of arts in history from California State University, Northridge. After teaching college-level American history, she moved into educational writing. She has authored books, textbooks, teacher's guides, lessons, and assessment questions in the field of history. When she is not writing or reading, she enjoys travel, photography, and hiking with her dogs. Her blog features her travel adventures and latest fiction projects.

Katy Schiel is a writer and artist who lives in the Boston area with her husband and two cats. She studied history at the University of Massachusetts at Amherst after spending a few years wandering through Europe.

# PHOTO CREDITS

Cover (newspaper) William West/AFP/Getty Images; cover (Queen Elizabeth) WPA Pool/Getty Images; cover (coronation)© iStockphoto.com/duncan1890; p. 5 Max Mumby/Indigo/Getty Images;pp. 8, 14, 21 DEA/G. Dagli Orti/De Agostini/Getty Images; p. 10 Art Collection 2/Alamy Stock Photo; p. 16 Museo di Capodimonte, Naples, Campania, Italy/Bridgeman Images; p. 18 Universal Images Group/Getty Images; p. 20 Dave Head/Shutterstock.com; p. 24 PHAS/Universal Images Group/Getty Images; p. 25 Apic/Hulton Archive /Getty Images; p. 27 DEA Picture Library/De Agostini/Getty Images; p. 28 mountainpix/Shutterstock.com; p. 31 National Archives and Records Administration; p. 33 The Metropolitan Museum of Art, Ann and George Blumenthal Fund, 1950, [50.58.4]; p. 35 Michael Bowles/Getty Images; p. 36 The United Kingdom Parliamentary Archives; p. 38 Takashi Images /Shutterstock.com; p. 41 Photo Josse/Leemage/Corbis Historical/Getty Images; p. 42 Musee de la Ville de Paris, Musee Carnavalet, Paris, France /Bridgeman Images; p. 45 Henry Guttmann/Hulton Royals Collection/Getty Images; p. 46 Hulton-Deutsch/Corbis Historical/Getty Images; p. 47 Official White House Photo by Shealah Craighead; chapter opener pages (world map silhouette) Vectorios2016/DigitalVision Vectors/Getty Images.

Design and Layout: Nicole Russo-Duca; Photo Researcher: Nicole DiMella